A Holiday to Remember

I Talk You Talk Press

CONTENTS

THE BEGINNING

CHRYSA

"I don't want to marry Michalis!" shouted Chrysa.

Chrysa's mother was very surprised. "But Chrysa, he is a nice boy! We know his family. He loves you! Why don't you want to marry him?"

Chrysa looked out of the window. "I don't want to get married yet. And I don't love Michalis."

Her mother sighed. "Chrysa! Chrysa! Michalis' father spoke to your father about you and Michalis. Michalis spoke to your father too. He wants to marry you. Your father is very pleased. They are a good family. Your father will be very angry with you if you say 'no'. Please say 'yes'. Please say you will marry Michalis."

"No. This is my life, and I want to do things before I get married. Mama, please understand. If I marry Michalis, his family will want us to have a child very soon. I will have a big house and money, but no freedom."

"Of course," said her mother. "You will have a good house, and no money worries. Michalis' family is rich."

"Well, Mama. We are rich too. But I want to travel. I want to meet different people. Please tell Papa I will think about marrying Michalis. But first, I want to have some freedom. Ask him to let me go away for a while. I want to meet some new people. I want to have fun."

"Chrysa. I understand. I will ask your father. But he will be very angry."

"I don't care. If he says 'no', I'll go anyway!"

JARMO

Jarmo sat in his apartment in Helsinki. He was looking at his computer screen. He was reading an email from his girlfriend Vilma.

He could not believe it.

---*Dear Jarmo,*

I'm sorry. Last week I went to an international student meeting in Vaasa. I met a guy from Uppsala University. Since we met, we have spent all our free time together. His name is Sten. He is a wonderful person. Sten has invited me to stay with his family in Sweden during the university vacation. I have decided to go. I know that we planned to go camping together during the vacation, but then I met Sten. I am very happy, but I don't want you to be sad. I hope you will find something nice to do during the vacation. I hope you can meet some nice girls, and find a new girlfriend.

We had some nice times together. I like you very much, but I like Sten more. I'm sorry, but this is goodbye. Vilma---

Jarmo was very upset. He picked up a picture of himself and Vilma from his desk. He threw it at the wall. He stood up and shouted. He walked up and down the room. After a while, he calmed down.

If Vilma can treat me like this, she is not a nice person. I am better without a girlfriend. I worked very hard at my part-time job so I could take Vilma on a vacation. I will take a holiday by myself, he thought. *I will go to France!*

AKINA

Akina and Mie were drinking coffee in a restaurant near Shinjuku Station in Tokyo. They were both very excited.

"The day after tomorrow we'll be on the plane!" said Mie. "I can't believe it!"

"And the day after that, we'll join the adventure tour group in Paris!" said Akina. She smiled. "I can't wait!"

Akina and Mie had just graduated from university. The other students in their class were taking a graduation trip to Singapore. They had reserved rooms for three nights in a five star hotel. They planned to go sightseeing and shopping. Akina and Mie wanted to do something different. They found out about adventure tours for young people. They chose a cycling tour in France. It was not expensive. They found very cheap airfares. Their adventure would cost only a little more than their classmates' vacation in Singapore.

They finished their coffee and paid the man at the counter.

"Oh no! It's raining," said Akina, looking out of the door of the restaurant. "We're going to get wet!"

"Let's run," said Mie.

The two friends ran towards the railway station.

Then disaster! Mie fell over. Akina knelt on the ground next to her.

"Mie! Are you OK?"

Mie's eyes were filled with tears. "My ankle. It hurts a lot!"

Mie could not stand up. People gathered around the two young women. A man knelt down next to Akina.

"I am a doctor. Take off her shoe, please. Let me take a look," he said.

The doctor examined Mie's ankle.

"You need to go to hospital," he said. "I can't be sure, but I think you have broken your ankle."

The next morning, Akina went to visit Mie in hospital.

"I talked to the travel agent," she said. "We have travel insurance. So you're OK. You had an accident. So the insurance company will give you your money back."

"What about you, Akina?" asked Mie.

"It doesn't matter about me," answered Akina.

"They won't give you your money back, will they?" said Mie.

"It doesn't matter," said Akina.

"Yes it does!" Mie was upset. "You must go. Go alone. You'll be OK!"

"I can't go without you. This was our dream," said Akina.

"We can go away together another time. Please go. You can speak English very well, and you will meet people on the tour. I am sure they will speak English too. I had an accident, so I will get all my money back. But if you cancel, you won't get your money back. Just go!"

HEHU

Kahu Rakena put the food on the table and sat down opposite her two eldest sons. She watched them eating. She was very proud of them.

They are both so handsome, she thought. When her husband died in a tractor accident four years ago, Ihapa left his job in the city, and

Hehu left university. They came home to run the farm.

The farm was doing well, but she worried that Ihapa and Hehu were working too hard, and having no fun, especially Hehu.

Hehu was much bigger than his older brother and very strong. But he was shy and very quiet.

"Aren't you going to eat, Mum?" asked Ihapa.

"Yes. But I want to talk to you first."

"Ihapa, you had a holiday in Australia at Christmas, so now it's Hehu's turn. The twins and Missy and Hine will be home for the school holidays next month. They can help on the farm. So Hehu can have a holiday."

Ihapa nodded. "It's a good idea Mum. Hehu, you need to get away and enjoy life for a while. You should take a break."

Hehu shook his head. "There is too much to do on the farm."

"No," said Ihapa. "The twins get lazy at school. It will be good for them to work. And they must learn how to look after the farm. We will manage very well. You go on a holiday."

"No," said Hehu. "I don't want a holiday."

Kahu is a great mother, but she is also tough. "Hehu. I'm telling you. Take a holiday!"

All Kahu's children know, that when Kahu talks like that, you can't say 'no'.

Hehu sighed. "OK."

"Where would you like to go?" asked Ihapa.

Hehu looked at the ceiling. He looked at the food on his plate. Then he said very slowly, "I would like to go to Europe."

PACHAI

One evening in March, Pachai came back to the big, beautiful apartment near Place Victor Hugo in Paris. Pachai lived with his uncle, who was a famous doctor. Pachai was studying to be a doctor too. His uncle was in the dining room. He was holding a large envelope.

"Ah, Pachai. I have told Basma that we will eat dinner a little late tonight. I want to talk to you first. Sit down."

Pachai sat down at the dining table. His uncle sat down opposite him and put the envelope on the table in front of him.

"You did very well in your final exams," said his uncle. "I am very pleased with you. All the family is very pleased with you. Now you have to spend time working in a hospital before you can become a doctor."

"Yes, Uncle," said Pachai. He was puzzled. What did his uncle want to talk about?

"Your mother has been sending emails to me, and talking on the telephone. She is sure you will become a very important doctor. So she is looking for a good wife for you. She has found some young women in Gujarat who might be possible."

Pachai's uncle pointed to the envelope on the table. "All the information about them is here," he said.

"But Uncle!" Pachai was shocked. "I don't want my mother to find a wife for me!"

"Pachai!" His uncle was angry. "It is our custom. You must trust your mother to find the right wife for you!"

"But Uncle! I have lived here in Paris with you for almost six years. You and Aunt Basma know me better than my mother."

"But we are here in Paris. You must marry a young woman who was born and educated in India. We can advise your mother, but we can't help her to find a wife for you. I suppose you want to find a wife yourself. I suppose you want to fall in love!"

"I know I must marry. I know I must marry a woman from our culture, but it would also be nice to marry a woman I loved!"

His uncle smiled. "My mother chose Basma for me. The first time I saw Basma, I fell in love with her. My mother was very wise and very clever."

"Uncle," said Pachai. "I love my mother. I love you and Aunt Basma. You have been very good to me. I will marry. I will do the right thing. But please Uncle, not yet. I have been studying very hard. I haven't had any fun. Can I have some time before I marry?"

"I understand, Pachai," answered his uncle. "Perhaps your mother is hurrying you too much. I will talk to her. I will tell her you are very young for marriage. I will ask her to wait a little. And of course you are tired after so much study. Your hospital training doesn't start until September. Why don't you take a vacation? I will pay for it. We will say it is a graduation present."

"Thank you Uncle," said Pachai.

SHELLEY
Shelley is Australian. She was working at a school in East London.

It was a special school for children with learning problems. She loved her job, and was very good at it. Shelley shared an apartment with Fiona. Fiona was from Ireland, and she was a nurse. Shelley loved living in London. It was a great experience, but sometimes she got homesick. Every night when she got home from work, she turned on her computer. There were often new Facebook postings, or emails from her friends in Sydney. One night, when she checked her email after work, there was a very exciting message.

"Fiona!" she shouted. "Come and look at this email!" Fiona was cooking dinner. She turned the oven off and went into the tiny living room.

"What is it?" she asked.

"Look! It's an email from my cousin Hehu. He's coming to Europe for a vacation! He is coming for a month! I can't wait to see him! Is it OK if he stays here?"

"Uh, I guess so," said Fiona. "But the apartment's very small. Where will he sleep?"

"He can sleep here in the living room."

"Well, you are a tiny person. I guess if he is small like you, it might be OK."

Shelley laughed. "He's a very big person! But I am sure he can sleep on the floor. I'll show you a photograph!"

Shelley opened a photo file and showed Fiona a picture. It was a family group. They were on a beach.

"That's Aunty Kahu," said Shelley pointing to a very beautiful middle-aged woman sitting in a chair. "And then my cousins, Hine, Mare, everyone calls her Missy, Koha and Tane. Koha and Tane are twins. Then Ihapa and Hehu are standing at the back."

"Which one's Hehu?" asked Fiona.

"The taller one," said Shelley. Fiona looked closely at the photograph on the computer screen.

"Wow," she said. "Those guys are so good looking. If Hehu is as handsome as his photograph, then of course he can come to stay!"

"He won't be here all the time," said Shelley. "He wants to see Europe. I will take some vacation, and maybe I can go somewhere with him. So maybe he will only stay for a few nights. Are you sure it's OK?"

"Of course," said Fiona.

Shelley is so excited, she thought. *She must miss her family and friends very much.*

But Fiona was puzzled. "Shelley," she said. "Maybe it is rude to ask you, but those people in the photograph are all very tall. You are so tiny and you have very pale skin and red hair."

Shelley laughed. "I know," she said. "And they have black hair, brown eyes and much darker skin than I have. That's because they are pure Maori. I am only half Maori. Aunty Kahu's husband and my father were brothers. My mother's Australian and I look like her. She's short and has red hair too. After my father died, my mother had to work very hard to make money, so she often sent me to New Zealand to stay with Aunty Kahu and Uncle Hemi. I spent many school vacations on the farm. When I was at university, Uncle Hemi died too. He was killed in a tractor accident. Ihapa is two years older than me, and Hehu and I are the same age. They are like my brothers, but maybe better, because we never fight with each other."

1. ONE MORNING IN PARIS

It was 8:50am on a warm early summer morning in Paris. A tall man and a woman with short red hair were walking down a small side street near the Sorbonne. They were wearing shorts and T-shirts and carrying backpacks. The man pointed to a sign on a window across the street.

"Action and Adventure Tours," he said. "That's it."

"Good," said the red-haired woman. "We're in the right place. Look. There are other people waiting."

"Maybe they are going to join the same tour as us," said the man.

They joined the small group outside the tour company's office.

"Hi," said the woman. "It's a nice morning, isn't it?"

The tall man put his backpack on the ground, and smiled at everyone. *If these people are joining the same tour as us, we will be together for a week,* he thought. *I wonder if they are friendly people.*

There was another woman in the little group. She was small and had long dark hair. She was holding a folder of papers and a map of Paris. She was looking at the sign on the office window of the adventure tour company and checking the papers in her folder. She was wearing jeans and a pink jacket. Next to her were two men. One was very thin. He had a big canvas bag on his shoulder. He was wearing jeans and a shirt. The sleeves of his shirt were rolled up. The other man was shorter. He was dressed all in black. His blond hair was cut very short. He was leaning against the window reading a book.

Just before 9:00am, a taxi stopped on the street in front of them, and a young woman got out. She had long blonde hair. Her clothes looked very stylish, and very expensive. She paid the driver, and carried her bag over to where the other young people were standing. She smiled.

"Good morning," she said.

Everyone smiled back.

The door of the tour company's office opened at exactly 9:00am, and a man came out, closing the door behind him. He was carrying a plastic folder filled with papers.

"Are you the people for the bicycle tour of Provence?" he asked.

"Yes, I am one of them," answered the blond man dressed in black. "I'm Jarmo Virtanen. I guess these other people are going on the bicycle tour too."

Jarmo looked around at the rest of the group. Everyone smiled and nodded.

The man took a piece of paper from the folder and looked at it.

"There should be seven of you," said the man. "Someone is late."

The small woman in the pink jacket spoke. "I think maybe that's my friend. She had an accident in Tokyo three days ago. She broke her ankle, so she couldn't come."

"I see," said the man. "Is her name Akina Tanaka?"

"No. I'm Akina Tanaka. My friend's name is Mie Kobayashi."

"OK," said the man with the folder.

"Where is the minibus?" asked the woman with the red hair. "I thought we were leaving for Nimes at nine o'clock."

"Uh, yes. Well, there's a problem," said the man. "Your cycling tour has been cancelled."

"What! Why?"

"Well as you know, our cycle tours provide bicycles for everyone. We take you by bus to Nimes, and you meet the truck with the bicycles. Then we use the truck to carry your bags to your hotels. The problem is that our truck with the bicycles inside was stolen last night. We have no bicycles for you."

Everyone looked very disappointed.

"I'm very sorry," said the man. "But we can't do anything. The police are looking for the truck, but it might take them a long time to find it. And all the cycles might have been sold. But you will all get your money back."

"Good," said the red-haired woman. "At least we can do

something else."

The man took some more papers from his folder. "Some of you booked your tour with us directly, and paid by credit card," he said. "That's Jarmo Virtanen, Chrysa Melias and Pachai Mehta. Shelley and Hehu Rakena paid for their tour through a travel agent in London. Is that right?"

"Yes," said the red-haired woman.

The man read some more papers. "And Mie Kobayashi and Akina Tanaka made their reservation in Tokyo, and paid a travel agent there."

"That's correct," said Akina.

"The people who paid by credit card will get a credit on their card. It will take three to four weeks. I'm afraid the people who booked through a travel agent will have to go back to that agency to get their money back."

"But I have a cheap air ticket from New Zealand," said the tall man. "I can't change it. My flight back to New Zealand is in seven days' time. What am I going to do until then?"

"I'm sorry. I don't know," said the tour agent. "But there is nothing we can do. Here is a letter for each of you. It explains that the cycle tour was cancelled. You should take it to your travel agent. You will have no trouble getting your money back, but it will take a few weeks."

He handed a letter to each person. Then he went back inside the agency and closed the door.

The six young people stood outside the agency and looked at each other.

"This is terrible," said Jarmo. "I am very angry."

"It's not their fault," said the man from New Zealand. "But it is a problem for Shelley and me. We don't have enough money to stay in Paris for a week. But I really want to spend some time in France."

The thin man carrying the big canvas bag spoke. "There is a coffee shop across the road. Why don't we go there? We can talk about it."

"Good idea," said the red-haired woman. "I'm Shelley, by the way."

She picked up her backpack and started walking towards the coffee shop. The three men followed her.

Akina didn't move. The beautiful blonde woman spoke to her.

"Are you OK?"

"I'm wondering what to do," said Akina. "This is the first time I have been outside Japan."

The blonde woman touched her arm. "My name is Chrysa. Everyone has the same problem. But I think we will feel better after we have a cup of coffee. Why don't we join the others?"

Akina smiled. "OK."

Chrysa and Akina walked across the road and into the coffee shop.

"Over here," called Shelley. She was sitting at a big round table. "The guys are getting coffee for all of us."

Soon the three men came over to the table. They were each carrying two cups of coffee. When everyone was sitting down and drinking their coffee, Jarmo said, "OK. This is bad news for everyone. What we can do to help each other?"

2. DOES ANYONE HAVE A GOOD IDEA?

"Let's introduce ourselves first. I'm Jarmo. I'm Finnish. I'm a final year student at university. I hope to become a famous writer one day. But I have very little money. I worked in a bar for six months to pay for a vacation. I spent all my money on this tour. I have just enough money to go back to Finland, but I don't want to. I start classes in two weeks, and I really want to have a holiday first!"

"I'm Pachai. I come from Gujarat in India, but I'm living with my uncle here in Paris. I just finished my courses at a medical university, and my uncle gave me this trip as a graduation present. I was looking forward to it very much."

The red-haired woman spoke next. "I'm Shelley, and it's nice to meet you. I'm Australian, but I'm living in London for a while. I have a job teaching young children with learning problems. This big, quiet guy sitting next to me is Hehu. He came to visit me all the way from New Zealand. We had a great time sightseeing in England. Then we spent a lot of Hehu's holiday money, and most of my spare cash on this trip. I can go back to my apartment in London, but it seems a pity."

Jarmo looked surprised. "So Hehu is not your husband?"

Hehu laughed. "No. Shelley's my cousin."

"But you don't look the same." Jarmo looked embarrassed. "Oh, sorry. That was rude."

"That's OK," said Hehu. He smiled. "You're right. She's small

12

and red-haired, and I'm big, with black hair and brown skin. But we are cousins."

"What do you do, Hehu?" asked Pachai.

"I'm a farmer."

Hehu turned to Akina. "It's your turn," he said.

"I'm Akina. I just finished university. My friend Mie and I planned this trip. But she had an accident, and couldn't come. The air tickets were very cheap, and if I cancelled my trip, I wouldn't get any money back. So my friend told me to come alone. But I am worried now. I will have to find a cheap hotel, but I don't know if I have enough money to last a week."

The beautiful blonde woman spoke next. "I'm Chrysa. I come from Greece. I usually take vacations with my parents. I thought it was a great idea to go on an adventure tour with young people. I could go home. But I'm like Jarmo. I don't want to."

Nobody asked Chrysa about her job. Chrysa was pleased. She didn't want to say that she didn't have a job, and had never had one. She didn't want to say that she only stayed home with her mother, went shopping, and went to restaurants and parties.

They wouldn't understand, she thought.

"So. Some of us need a place to stay until we can take our flights home. And everyone wants a holiday," said Jarmo. "A very cheap holiday."

"Could we do something together?" asked Pachai. "Is there something very cheap we could all do together for a week?"

"What a great idea!" said Shelley. She was excited. "How much money do we have?"

"I have about three hundred euros," said Hehu. "But that has to last until I get back to Auckland."

"I have about the same," said Shelley.

Akina had a little more money. "I have five hundred and fifty euros," she said. "But I have to spend some of that on presents for my friends and family."

"Can everyone find three hundred euros?" asked Jarmo.

"I can," said Pachai. "How about you, Chrysa?"

I have thousands of euros, thought Chrysa. *I could pay for everyone to have a holiday in a good hotel. But I don't want to. They are nice and friendly. I think they are interesting. I want them to be my friends, but I don't want them to know I am rich. I don't want to be different from them.*

"Yes. I have three hundred," she answered.

"Why don't we all look on the Internet?" said Pachai. "Like a competition! Let's see who can find the best holiday for six people for a week, for only one thousand eight hundred euros."

Jarmo took his mini iPad out of his bag. Everyone else took out their smart phones.

"OK, everyone," said Jarmo. "We have thirty minutes to find a cheap vacation."

3. DOES EVERYONE AGREE?

Akina didn't do any Internet searching. She signed onto her email account.

I'll send an email to my parents and one to Mie, she thought. But then she didn't.

They will worry a lot, she thought. *I will send them an email when there is a plan.*

She sat and looked at her phone.

I don't know these people. They are from different countries. They all seem very strong and confident. I like them. I want to go on vacation with them.

Chrysa didn't search on the Internet either. She didn't know how to plan a cheap holiday.

I can't help, but I can buy coffee, she thought. *I will buy another coffee for everyone.* She came back with a tray of coffees.

"Ooh! More coffees!" said Shelley. "Thank you, Chrysa."

Hehu was sitting next to Akina. He passed a cup of coffee to her and smiled.

He's so nice, thought Akina. *He is so big, but he is so quiet and gentle. These people are kind. I feel safe with them.*

After 30 minutes, Jarmo said, "Stop."

"Did anyone find anything good?" asked Jarmo.

"Did you find anything, Hehu?" asked Pachai.

"No. Sorry. Everything I looked at was too expensive, or already fully booked."

"The same with me," said Shelley. "I found some great tours, but they were all too expensive."

"I couldn't find anything either," said Pachai.

Jarmo was smiling. "I had an idea", he said. "I hope you like it. Why don't we rent a house?"

"A house?" Shelley was very surprised. "Why should we rent a house?"

"Well, I found a special house," said Jarmo. He put his mini iPad on the table. "Look! Here is the advertisement, and there are some pictures!"

The pictures were of a big stone house. It was in the middle of a garden. The garden was next to a beach.

"It has six bedrooms, a tennis court and a swimming pool. It's a vacation rental house. The owners provide bicycles and canoes. It's perfect!" Jarmo was very proud.

"But Jarmo," said Chrysa. "A vacation house like this will be expensive."

"Usually, yes. But read the advertisement. It says the house is only available for one week from today! Someone was renting it, but they had to go home a week early. So it is available for this week for only four hundred and fifty euros. It is a seventy-five percent discount!"

"Uh, where is it?" asked Hehu.

"It's in Brittany. Near a place called Saint-Brieuc. We can catch a bus or a train, and we could be there tonight," said Jarmo.

"We all planned to go on a cycling tour. An adventure tour. If we rent this house, we can cycle, canoe, swim, or play tennis! It's perfect!" Pachai was excited.

Suddenly everyone else was excited too.

"Let's do it!" said Shelley. "Does everyone agree?"

"Yes!" said everyone. "Let's rent this house! Let's spend a week in Brittany!"

4. MAKING PLANS

Jarmo opened his backpack and took out a pen and a notebook.

"We need to make plans. So, what do we need to do?"

"We can make a reservation for the house on the Internet," said Pachai. "But we will have to pay for the house and get the keys. It might be easier to telephone the company. I can do that."

"Good idea," said Jarmo.

"Yes, do it," said Shelley.

"It's so noisy in here. I won't be able to hear anything. I'll go outside," said Pachai.

"We'll need to buy food and drink," said Chrysa. "The shops in holiday villages are sometimes very expensive. I think we should make a list and then find a big supermarket. It will be cheaper."

"Here in Paris?" asked Hehu.

"No. I think we should find somewhere nearer to the house. We don't want to carry boxes and bags around Paris."

"Let's make a list while we are waiting for Pachai."

Chrysa took a tiny gold pen and a slim diary out of her handbag.

"Six people for seven days. We will need a lot of food. Does anyone have any food allergies or special food needs?"

Shelley waved her hand at Chrysa.

"Sorry, Chrysa. I'm vegetarian. Will that be a problem?"

"Not at all. How about cheese and milk? And eggs? Are they OK?"

"Yes, no problem. But Chrysa, maybe we should ask Pachai too. Didn't he say he came from Gujarat? I think that almost everyone in that part of India is vegetarian."

"OK, we'll ask him. Does anyone else have any special food needs or allergies?"

Jarmo, Akina and Hehu all said 'no'.

"What do you all like to eat for breakfast? Do you think we will have barbecues? We must find somewhere near the house to buy milk and bread every day," said Chrysa.

Chrysa started making a long list. Shelley was very impressed.

"Wow, Chrysa! You are an expert at this."

Chrysa's face turned pink. "Thank you. My mother has a lot of parties. I have to help her."

"Lucky for us!" said Hehu.

Pachai came back into the café. "Everything is organized," he said. "We are lucky. It is a national company. Normally we would have to go to Saint-Malo to get the keys. But the family, who moved out early, lives in Paris. They returned the keys to the Paris office this morning. We can go and get them there. We have to pay the rental fee at the same time."

"We must decide how to get to the house," said Chrysa. "Maybe we should hire a car, or a van."

"Or take a bus," said Shelley.

"The company told me on the telephone that there is a direct train from Montparnasse to Saint-Brieuc. They have a special young persons' ticket. If you are under twenty-five, it costs seventy euros for a round trip. Is anyone older than that? No one? Good. Then there is a very good local bus service. The bus goes past the gate of the house. If we ask the bus driver, he will stop the bus for us. So we only have to carry our bags from the road to the house," said Pachai.

"That sounds good," said Jarmo.

"Do you think there will be a big supermarket in Saint-Brieuc?" asked Chrysa. "We can do our food shopping there before we catch the bus."

"I am sure there will be," said Pachai. "Are you planning to buy all the food for the week?"

"Yes. I have been making a list. Shelley said maybe you are vegetarian."

"Yes," said Pachai. "That is true. But in my family we eat some dairy products and eggs."

"We will all look at the food in the supermarket. You can choose the things that you like to eat."

"Well then," said Jarmo. "Pachai. You are the French speaker. So will you go to the company and pay the rental fee?"

"No problem," said Pachai. "I'll get the keys. I hope they will give me some maps too. Akina, would you like to come with me?"

Akina was surprised. She felt shy because she didn't know anything about renting holiday homes. Everyone else seemed very confident.

It is nice of Pachai to ask me to go with him, she thought.

"Oh, yes. I would like to go with you. Thank you," she said.

"The rest of us will go to Montparnasse station and buy the tickets. We will meet you there later," said Jarmo. "We need the money to pay for the house. Seventy-five euros each, please. And money for the rail tickets. That's seventy euros."

Everyone took out money. They each gave 75 euros to Pachai and 70 euros to Jarmo.

"Thanks," said Jarmo. "I hope someone at the train ticket office speaks English."

"I am sure there will be an English speaker there," said Shelley. "But if not, it doesn't matter. Hehu speaks good French. Where will we meet at the railway station?"

"In front of the ticket office is a good place," said Chrysa. "Pachai and Akina, when do you think you can get there?"

"It's eleven am now," said Pachai. "I don't know how long it will take, but I am sure we can be there by three pm."

"OK, everyone. We have a plan," said Jarmo. "Let's go."

5. WE'RE ON OUR WAY TO BRITTANY!

Hehu helped Jarmo buy the tickets at the railway station. It didn't take very long. They bought tickets for the 3:20pm train.

"I hope Pachai and Akina aren't late." Chrysa was worried.

"Oh, I am sure they will be here in plenty of time," said Shelley. The four young people found a cheap café in the station. They ordered bread rolls with cheese. They tasted very good. They found a shop and bought snacks and bottled water for the train trip. At 2:45 they were waiting in front of the ticket office. They did not have to wait long. Pachai and Akina came into the station. They were both smiling.

"Everything is fine," said Pachai. "We had enough time to eat lunch."

"Let's find the platform for our train," said Shelley.

Everyone enjoyed the train trip to Saint-Brieuc. The countryside was very flat. They could see farms and small villages across the wide fields. They passed cities too. The biggest was Chartres. Hehu told Akina about the cathedral there.

"It is very big and old," he said. "I would like to see it one day."

About 30 minutes after they passed Chartres, the train suddenly stopped. There was an announcement:

'There is a problem on the railway line. We are sorry for the delay.'

The train was stopped for almost two hours. Jarmo read his book. Hehu taught Akina and Shelley some words and phrases in French. Chrysa and Pachai talked about food and cooking. After a while, Chrysa became worried.

"We will arrive in Saint-Brieuc much later than we planned. We have to go shopping, and then catch the bus to the house. The house is about fourteen kilometres from Saint-Brieuc. It will be dark when we arrive there," she said.

"I don't think so," said Pachai. "It won't be dark until about nine pm. We will be at the house long before that, I'm sure."

Finally they arrived in Saint-Brieuc. They carried their bags out of the station and onto the street. Pachai asked directions to the nearest supermarket. There was one about ten minutes' walk away. It took about an hour to buy food and walk back to the station. They found the bus stops near the train station, and looked at the timetable.

"Oh no," said Chrysa. "We just missed our bus. We have to wait thirty minutes for the next one."

It was a warm evening and they enjoyed sitting on the benches near the bus stop, watching the local people. When the bus arrived, they got on with all their baggage and supermarket bags. They were the only passengers. Pachai showed the address to the driver.

"The holiday house company told us that you would stop the bus at the gate to the house. Is that OK?" he asked.

"Of course," said the bus driver. "It's no problem. There are many big houses around that area. But usually the people who stay in them come in expensive cars!"

The bus ride seemed to take a long time. It was now very dark outside. Eventually, the bus stopped in a narrow country road.

"There's the entrance," said the bus driver.

Pachai got off the bus and looked at the entrance. It was an old brick arch. The gate inside the arch was rusty and broken.

"Are you sure this is the house?" asked Pachai. "It doesn't look like the photographs on the Internet."

The bus driver laughed.

"The holiday house company wants you to rent the house! Of course they only put up beautiful photographs! Maybe the photographs were taken twenty years ago. Now please hurry and take all your bags off my bus. This is my last bus run today. I want to go home and eat."

They carried their bags to the side of the road, and the bus disappeared into the darkness.

"Come on," said Jarmo. "We are all tired and we need to take everything into the house."

He opened his bag and took out a torch. He looked through the arch. There was a rough path, wide enough for a car.

"It's very dark," he said. "Maybe I should go first and light the way for you."

He picked up his backpack and some of the supermarket bags, and walked through the arch.

Hehu picked up his backpack and most of the other food bags.

"You can't carry all of that!" said Chrysa.

Hehu laughed. "Of course I can. Working on a farm makes you strong." He walked through the entrance towards Jarmo.

Pachai and Shelley picked up their baggage and the rest of the shopping bags. They disappeared down the path.

Chrysa looked at Akina. "Are you OK?" she asked.

"I'm fine," said Akina. "But it is so dark and strange. I think it's scary."

"I think it's scary too," said Chrysa. "But it's just because we are tired. It has been a very long day."

Chrysa and Akina picked up their bags and walked through the archway. They followed the others along the rough path. It curved to the left. When they walked round the curve, they saw the house.

6. THE HOUSE

"Is this it?" asked Shelley. "It looks so much smaller and older than the house in the photographs."

Pachai took the papers from the holiday house company out of his bag. Jarmo shone the torch on the papers. Everyone gathered around.

"I don't know," said Jarmo. "Maybe it is the house in the photographs. It's too late to call the holiday house company."

"Well it's made of stone. And it has two floors and shutters on the windows. It must be the same house," said Chrysa.

"The bus driver said this is the place," said Shelley. "Let's knock on the door. If it is the wrong house, maybe there is someone inside and they can help us find the right house."

They walked towards the back door of the house. Pachai knocked on the door. They were all surprised because the door opened.

"It wasn't locked. It wasn't even closed properly," said Pachai.

Inside the door was a small room with a stone floor. There was another door opposite the back door. It was open and by the light of Jarmo's torch, they could see an old-fashioned kitchen. There was a big iron stove, a modern electric cooker, a large wooden table and an old sofa.

"Hello! Hello! Anyone there?" shouted Pachai. There was no answer.

"Maybe the people who were staying here left in a hurry. Maybe they forgot to lock the door," said Jarmo.

"The agent told Akina and me that the family had to leave very suddenly because the man's mother had a heart attack in Paris. They thought she would die soon," said Pachai. "So it's easy to understand that they forgot to close and lock the door."

"Let's go in," said Jarmo.

Hehu found a light switch near the back door and turned it on. Lights came on in the small entrance hall and the kitchen. They carried their bags into the kitchen and looked around.

"They must have been in a great hurry," said Chrysa. "Look. They didn't even clean the kitchen."

She pointed to the big wooden table in the middle of the kitchen. There were dirty dishes on the table. She opened the door of the refrigerator. "And there's milk and other things in here."

"It's smaller and older than the photographs on the Internet, but the bus driver told us that holiday house companies often use old photographs. Maybe they even use photos of other houses," said Jarmo. "I think we should call the company tomorrow and complain, but we will have to stay here tonight. We don't have anywhere to go."

"I'm going to check the rest of the house," said Shelley. "I'll find the bedrooms. We're all tired. We need to eat and get some sleep."

There were narrow wooden stairs going upstairs from the kitchen. Shelley went up the stairs. The others could hear her walking above their heads. They started unpacking the bags of food, and finding plates and knives and forks so that they could eat. Chrysa made coffee. They put their food away in a large old wooden cupboard and in the refrigerator. Akina and Hehu put quiche and fruit on the table.

Shelley came back into the kitchen.

"It's a bit strange," she said. "There is a big bedroom at the front of the house. I don't think we should use that room. It seems to have someone's clothes and photographs and personal things in it."

"Sometimes people rent their houses to tourists only in the summer," said Chrysa. "They just move out and stay with relatives during the summer and make a lot of money. Maybe the owner of this house is doing that."

"Mmm," said Shelley. "Maybe that's true. I can only find two other bedrooms. They are very large. One has two double beds. I guess we girls can have that one and you guys can have the other bedroom. It has a normal bed and two camp beds in it. We won't be very comfortable, but I found sheets and blankets in a cupboard. I've made the beds. At least everything is very clean."

24

They ate a quick meal in the kitchen. No one spoke very much. Everyone was tired. They felt a little disappointed. The house was so different from the advertisement.

"Tomorrow will be a better day," said Hehu quietly. "The sun will be shining and we can call the holiday home rental company. I think we should go to bed and get a good night's sleep."

They cleaned the kitchen and took their backpacks upstairs.

"Goodnight," said Jarmo, Pachai and Hehu.

"Goodnight. See you in the morning," answered Akina, Chrysa and Shelley.

7. NOISES IN THE NIGHT

Akina and Shelley were sharing an old-fashioned double bed. Shelly woke up. *Something woke me up,* she thought. *A noise. I can still hear it. What's that noise? What is it?*

She sat up. It was a knocking noise. *Where is it coming from?* Shelley thought about the house. *The guys' room is above the kitchen. That front bedroom with all the clothes and things in it is above the living room. This bedroom must be above another room next to the kitchen. There was a door there, but we didn't open it last night.*

Shelley woke Akina up.

"What's the problem?" asked Akina. "Is something wrong?"

"Akina. Can you hear a noise downstairs?" asked Shelley.

"No, but I've been sleeping," answered Akina.

Chrysa spoke from the bed on the other side of the room. "I can hear it. Maybe there's an open door and it's banging in the wind."

"But I can't hear any wind outside," said Shelley. "Maybe an animal, like a dog or a cat, is down there. I think we should go and look."

Chrysa climbed out of bed and put a T-shirt on over her nightgown. She put on a pair of sandals. "OK. We won't get any sleep until we find out about the noise."

"Akina," said Shelley. "It's OK. Chrysa and I will go down and look. You can stay here."

Akina was very sleepy. She had not woken up properly. She couldn't hear the noise. "OK," she said and fell asleep again.

Chrysa smiled. "Akina is so tired. She had a long journey from

26

Japan. She was travelling for much longer than us."

Shelley was wearing shorts and a T-shirt. Her red hair was standing up in spikes all over her head. "I wish we had a torch. If we turn the lights on in the hallway and on the stairs, we will wake the others up."

"That's true," said Chrysa. "We won't turn the lights on up here, but we must turn on the stair lights. The stairs are so old and steep, we might fall down."

Chrysa and Shelley walked out of the bedroom quietly. It was very dark, so they used their hands to feel along the wall of the hallway. Chrysa walked into something. She screamed.

"It's only me." Chrysa heard Hehu's voice. "Can you hear the noise too? I'm going down to look."

The noise of Chrysa screaming woke Pachai and Jarmo. They switched on their bedroom light, and went out to the hallway.

"What's happening?" asked Jarmo.

"We don't know," answered Shelley. "We heard noises downstairs, and we were going down to look. Hehu heard them too. He moves like a cat, and we didn't know he was in the hallway until Chrysa walked into him."

Jarmo used his torch to find the light switches, and they all went along the hallway and down the narrow stairs into the kitchen.

"I think the noise is coming from over there," said Shelley pointing to the door at the end of the kitchen. They all stood quietly and listened.

"Stay here," said Hehu.

He walked across the kitchen and opened the door. He turned on a light. They could see an old-fashioned laundry room and a tall pile of boxes. Hehu went behind the boxes and disappeared. They all waited.

They heard the sound of a door opening. There was no sound for a while. Then Hehu appeared from behind the pile of boxes.

"Pachai," he said. "I think you should come."

Pachai went into the laundry room and Jarmo followed.

Chrysa and Shelley looked at each other.

"What is it?" asked Chrysa.

"I don't know. But maybe it's not good. Hehu looked very serious," said Shelley.

When Pachai and Jarmo followed Hehu behind the pile of boxes,

27

they saw an open door. The door was at the top of some very steep stone steps. There was a very weak light from a bulb hanging from a wire over the steps.

"Down here," said Hehu. "Be careful."

At the bottom of the steps was an old man. He was lying in a pool of red liquid. The red liquid was all over the floor.

Jarmo shone his torch on the man. "Is that blood? Is he dead?"

"No," said Hehu. "But he needs help."

Pachai pushed past Hehu and knelt down next to the man. He examined him carefully. "He's fallen and hit his head. He's unconscious. I don't think he has broken any bones."

"What's that red liquid then?" asked Jarmo.

"It's wine. He's been lying in it."

Jarmo looked around the room. It was a wine cellar. There were shelves of bottles and big plastic containers. Jarmo could see wine-making equipment everywhere.

"What was the noise we heard?" asked Jarmo.

Hehu pointed to the end of the room. There was a large metal container. Inside the container was a pump. The container was empty, but the pump was still moving. It was hitting the side of the metal container. On the floor was a large plastic bottle. The tube from the pump went into the bottle.

"I think he was pumping wine out of that metal container into the bottle. He fell and hit his head. He tried to get to the stairs but he lost consciousness. The pump didn't stop. It emptied the tank. When the bottle was full, the rest of the wine went onto the floor."

Pachai spoke again. "I think it is safe to move him. He has been lying in the wine for a long time on a stone floor. He is very cold. If we can get him up to the kitchen, I can examine him more closely. We can make him warm and call an ambulance. Do you think you can carry him, Hehu?"

"Of course."

"I'll move those boxes," said Jarmo. He went up the steps. After a few minutes, he said, "It's clear now."

At the bottom of the steps, Pachai moved out of the way to give Hehu space.

Hehu picked up the old man. Slowly and carefully, he carried him in his arms to the top of the steps. Pachai followed him.

8. I'LL SHOOT YOU!

Jarmo was in the kitchen telling Chrysa and Shelley about the old man and the accident. Hehu appeared carrying the old man, and Chrysa went to take the cushions off the sofa, so that Hehu could lay the old man down.

Suddenly the back door of the house opened and a man came into the kitchen. He was carrying a shotgun and it was pointing at them!

He was shouting in French. Only Hehu and Pachai could understand his words. But it didn't matter. Everyone understood that the man wanted to shoot them. No one moved.

Hehu was still holding the old man in his arms. He said something quietly in French to the man with the shotgun.

"What's Hehu saying?" Chrysa whispered to Pachai.

"He's telling the man with the shotgun that the old man is injured. That he must put him on the sofa. That the man with the gun must call for help. He must call for an ambulance.

"Now the man with the shotgun is saying it's a trick. That Hehu has killed the old man. He says that if Hehu moves, he will shoot him."

Chrysa thought maybe Hehu didn't understand, because he walked past the man with the gun, and put the old man gently on the sofa. He called Pachai to the sofa. Pachai went and checked the old man's pulse.

They are very brave, or very crazy, thought Chrysa.

The man with the gun was still shouting, but Pachai and Hehu didn't seem to notice.

Then Shelley saw Akina on the stairs. The man with the gun hadn't seen her. Shelley waved her hands at Akina. *Go back! Go back! Hide!*

Akina nodded and disappeared.

At least one of us might be safe, thought Shelley.

Pachai spoke to the man with the gun. Jarmo and Chrysa and Shelley tried to understand Pachai's words.

"He's saying something about danger," said Chrysa. He's talking about a telephone. And he said 'medecin'. I'm sure that's French for 'doctor'."

The man with the gun just shouted more. He was pointing the gun at Chrysa and Shelley.

"Chrysa. Shelley. Don't move." It was Hehu speaking. "He was angry before, but I didn't think he would shoot anyone. But now he is very angry. He doesn't believe us. He says the old man is his uncle. He thinks we are international criminals. He says we are probably selling drugs. He thinks we killed the old man. He says he will shoot you."

Chrysa and Shelley were very frightened. They looked at the man with the gun. Then they saw something very surprising. The back door was still open. There was a small person coming quietly through the doorway from outside. It was Akina! She was standing behind the man with the gun. Chrysa looked at the others. Pachai and Hehu were looking at the old man. They couldn't see anything, but Jarmo could see Akina. Jarmo was moving very slowly and carefully along the side of the table. Then Chrysa saw Jarmo had something in his hand behind his back. It was a bottle.

Suddenly everything happened at once. Jarmo threw the bottle at the gunman. The man turned quickly towards Jarmo, and Akina jumped forward. She kicked him in the back. He fell forward and dropped the shotgun.

Shelley ran forward and picked up the shotgun. Jarmo jumped on the man. He pushed him onto his face on the floor and pulled his arms behind his back.

The man started crying very loudly.

Jarmo said, "He smells very strongly of wine. I think he is very drunk."

Chrysa ran and hugged Akina. "You were amazing!" she said. "You saved us!"

Pachai called the police and the ambulance. The ambulance came and took the old man to hospital. The ambulance men thought he would be OK. The police came. They took the man and the shotgun too. But two policemen stayed at the house. They both spoke English. They wanted to see everyone's passports and travel tickets. They wanted to see the contract with the holiday house company. They wanted to hear the story from everyone. Finally, at about 5:00am, it seemed that the police believed them. There was only one part of the story they didn't believe. They couldn't believe that Akina had climbed out of a window and down the wall. They couldn't believe that she had kicked the gunman. They looked at her. She was wearing Hello Kitty pyjamas. She was so tiny, and she looked so young.

"How could you do it?" asked one of the policemen.

Akina was very sleepy but she tried to explain. "It was not so difficult. I am a karate black belt. I was a member of the university karate club."

The policemen went away. They said that everyone must stay inside the house. A policeman would stay outside the house. Someone would come back later, after everything was checked.

Everyone went upstairs and went back to bed.

"It was a strange start to our holiday!" said Jarmo to Hehu and Pachai.

Pachai didn't answer, he was already asleep.

Hehu laughed. "I wanted an interesting vacation, and I guess I'm getting one."

9. THE REAL HOLIDAY HOUSE

The policemen came back to the house in the middle of the afternoon. Chrysa and Jarmo had made some food, and everyone was sitting around the table eating and talking.

The policemen sat down at the table, and Chrysa gave them coffee.

"We have checked everything and we know that your story is true. We found the bus driver. He is very sorry. He made a mistake and stopped the bus at the wrong gate. The house you rented is about fifty metres along the road. We will help you move there. Of course it was good luck that you went to the wrong house. The owner of this house is Monsieur Jacques Villemont. He lives alone and doesn't like visitors. If you had not found him, probably he would have died. The doctors say he must stay in hospital for a few days but he will be OK."

"What about the man with the gun?" asked Jarmo.

"Yes. Poor Nils. He lives with his mother in a cottage near here. He had a bad car accident twenty years ago, and he has some mental problems. He has to take medicine. If he takes it, he is very calm. But his mother is getting old, and sometimes she doesn't check if he has taken his medicine. He has never been so dangerous before. We think he will have to live in a special home for people with problems like his. He won't trouble you again."

"That's a sad story," said Chrysa. "Is Monsieur Villemont really his uncle?"

"No, he isn't," answered the policeman. "Jacques Villemont's nephew was called Pierre. He died in the same car accident. Nils was driving. When Nils is normal, he feels very bad about it. I think that last night he thought he was Pierre. He was very drunk and very confused."

"You said that Monsieur Villemont doesn't like visitors," said Pachai. "But we would like to go and see him in the hospital. We would like to say we are sorry for coming into his house and staying here. Do you think that would be OK?"

The policeman smiled. "I am sure he would be pleased to see you. He knows he is a lucky man. He should thank you! Now, please pack everything and clean up here. Then we will take you to the real holiday house."

10. SIX DAYS WERE NOT ENOUGH

The real holiday house was wonderful. It looked exactly like the pictures on the Internet. They swam in the pool and went fishing. Jarmo taught everyone how to use the canoes. Akina learnt to play tennis. Chrysa showed Shelley and Pachai how to cook Greek food, and Hehu taught everyone how to do a real barbecue. They went to visit Monsieur Villemont in the hospital in Saint-Brieuc. The bus driver invited them to his home for a meal. They ate in cafes and drank in small local bars.

It was a very relaxing and happy holiday. But it was too short. On the last night, they sat on the beach and talked.

"I can't believe it," said Chrysa. "I have only known you all for a week, but I am going to miss you all so much."

"Me too," said Akina. "I was very nervous about coming to France alone, and in the beginning everything went wrong. But it was the best vacation ever."

"I will miss you all too," said Shelley. "But you know, we have become such good friends. We can meet somewhere and have another holiday together."

"That would be wonderful," said Chrysa. "Why don't we plan to do that?"

"It may not be so easy," answered Pachai. "Maybe some of us can get together sometime. But for all of us to meet might be very difficult."

Anyway, thought Pachai. *I can never do this once I am married.*

Jarmo was thinking the same thing. *These people have become important to me. Maybe if I get another part-time job I can save enough money to visit Pachai in Paris or Chrysa in Greece. But it will not be the same if we are not all together. Big, strong, quiet Hehu; energetic Shelley; clever and handsome Pachai; beautiful Chrysa; and cute and surprising Akina. Somehow we made something special.*

Everyone was very quiet. They sat and watched the moon travel across the sky and thought about going back to their normal lives.

"Oh, cheer up everyone!" said Shelley. She laughed. "You are all so sad. I would be sad too if I thought we wouldn't get together again. But I believe in magic and miracles, and I believe we will have another chance to do something like this."

The next day they said goodbye in Paris Montparnasse station. Everyone hugged each other. They exchanged email addresses and telephone numbers, and then it was time to go.

Hehu and Shelley left for the airport. As they walked away, Shelley turned around and shouted something.

"What did she say?" asked Jarmo.

"She said 'Until next time'," said Chrysa. She smiled.

Jarmo, Chrysa, Pachai and Akina held hands. "Until next time," they said together.

THANK YOU

Thank you for reading A Holiday to Remember. (Word count: 10,001) We hope you enjoyed it. The next book in the Holiday Club series is Together Again.

If you would like to read more graded readers, please visit our website http://www.italkyoutalk.com

Other Level 3 graded readers include
A Dangerous Weekend
Akiko and Amy Part 1
Akiko and Amy Part 2
Akiko and Amy Part 3
Be My Valentine
Different Seas
Enjoy Your Business Trip
Enjoy Your Homestay
I Need a Friend
Old Jack's Ghost Stories from England (1)
Old Jack's Ghost Stories from England (2)
Old Jack's Ghost Stories from Ireland
Old Jack's Ghost Stories from Japan
Old Jack's Ghost Stories from Scotland

Old Jack's Ghost Stories from Wales
Party Time!
Stories for Christmas
The Curse
Together Again
Who is Holly?

ABOUT THE AUTHOR

I Talk You Talk Press is a Japan-based publisher of language textbooks, graded readers and language learning/teaching resources.

Our team is made up of highly experienced language teachers and translators, who have all studied at least one additional language to an advanced level.

This experience enables us to design our materials from the perspective of both the teacher and the learner. We consult with both teachers and language learners when designing our textbooks and graded readers, and test our materials extensively in the classroom before publication.

We are a fast-growing press, and currently publish graded readers for learners of English. We publish new graded readers monthly.

www.ingramcontent.com/pod-product-compliance
Lightning Source LLC
Chambersburg PA
CBHW022348040426
42449CB00006B/768